Alfred's Premier Piano

Dennis Alexander • Gayle Kowalchyk • E. L. Lancaster • Victoria McArthur • Martha Mier

Level 2A continues the steady development of artistry and keyboard skills that began in 1A and continued through 1B.

- Note-reading skills are expanded to include treble notes E, F and G. Melodic and harmonic 6ths are used to help the student move freely around the keyboard.

- Eighth-note rhythm patterns are added to other rhythms of gradually increasing complexity.

- Technical *Workouts* continue the development of skills for playing hands together, hand-over-hand crossings and finger crossings.

Lesson Book 2A is designed to correlate with Theory and Performance Books 2A of *Alfred's Premier Piano Course.* When used together, they offer a fully integrated and unparalleled comprehensive approach to piano instruction.

To provide a performance model and a practice companion, a compact disc recording is included with the book. Each title is performed twice on acoustic piano—a *performance* tempo and a slower *practice* tempo.

See page 49 for information on the CD. Flash Cards 2A (22367) and a General MIDI Disk 2A (23260) are available separately.

Edited by Morton Manus

Cover Design by Ted Engelbart
Interior Design by Tom Gerou
Illustrations by Jimmy Holder
Music Engraving by Linda Lusk

Contents

Premier Music Review

1. Name the
   Landmark Notes.

2. On the blank lines below, name all the notes.

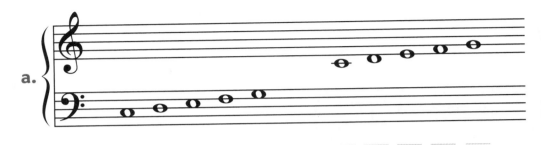

a.

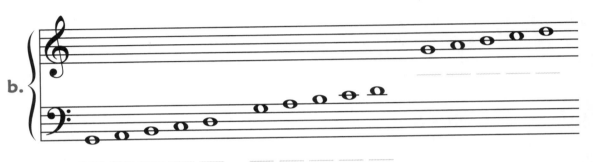

b.

3. Write **M** on the line next to each melodic interval and **H** next to each harmonic interval.
   Then connect each melodic and harmonic interval to its matching name.

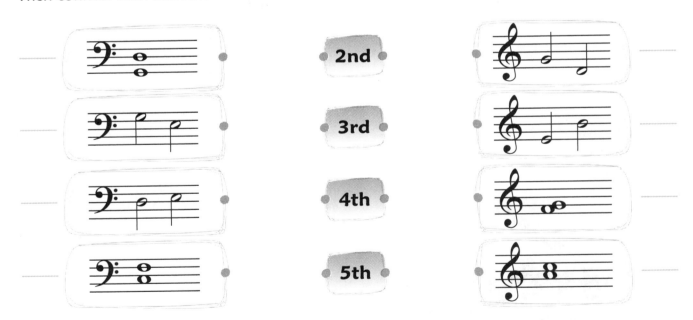

2nd

3rd

4th

5th

4. Write the counts (by measure) under the notes—then tap and count aloud.

5. Matching Game: Draw a line from the term or symbol in the middle to its matching example or definition.

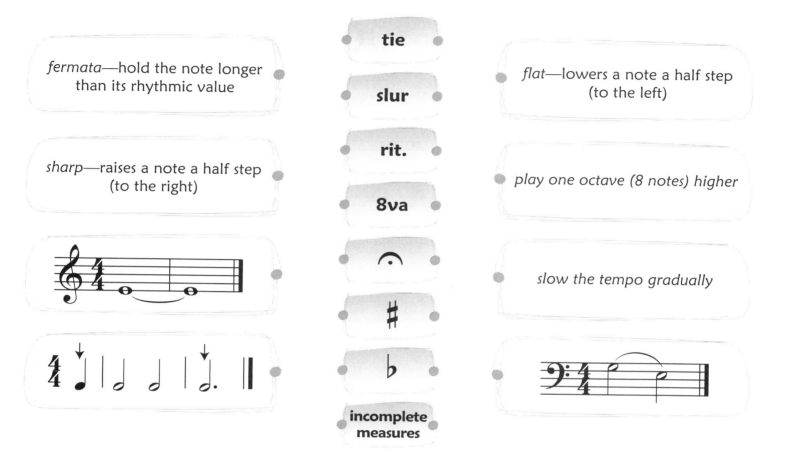

fermata—hold the note longer than its rhythmic value

sharp—raises a note a half step (to the right)

tie

slur

rit.

8va

𝄐

♯

♭

incomplete measures

flat—lowers a note a half step (to the left)

play one octave (8 notes) higher

slow the tempo gradually

6. Play this melody *legato* or *staccato*.
(circle one)

7. Play this melody *legato* or *staccato*.
(circle one)

8. Write the name on the correct black key for D♯, F♯ and G♯.

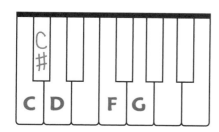

9. Write the name on the correct black key for E♭, A♭ and B♭.

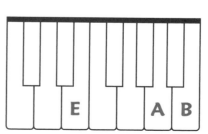

On with the Show!

* In this book, a red finger number indicates
that the hand moves up or down.

Duet: Student plays one octave higher.

**Optional: The half notes in the left hand of measures 1–6 may be played as a tremolo.

Moving Up from Treble C

for the C 5-finger Pattern

Treble C and the four notes that step up from it are called the *C 5-finger pattern*.

Stepping Up

Skipping Up

- Starting with Treble C, point to each note as you say its name aloud.
- Play with the RH and say the note names aloud.

Twinkling Skyline

Workout 1 **Hands Together**

Play 3 times each day.

Name notes.

Gently

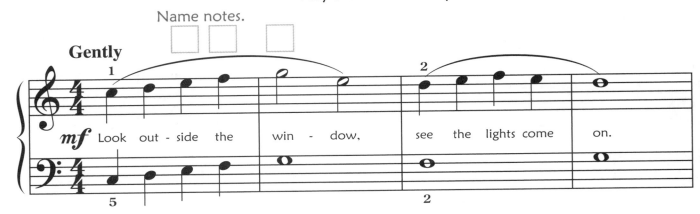

mf Look out-side the win - dow, see the lights come on.

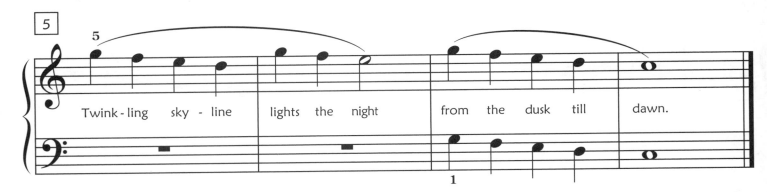

Twink-ling sky - line lights the night from the dusk till dawn.

Duet: Student plays LH **two** octaves higher and RH one octave higher.

Gently

CD 3/4
GM 2

Bartók's Study
(First Term at the Piano)

Béla Bartók (1881–1945) was born in Hungary and first studied piano with his mother. As an adult, he went into the countryside to record folk music of the Hungarian people. This folk music had a great influence on his compositions. Bartók spent the last years of his life in the United States.

Moderately

Béla Bartók

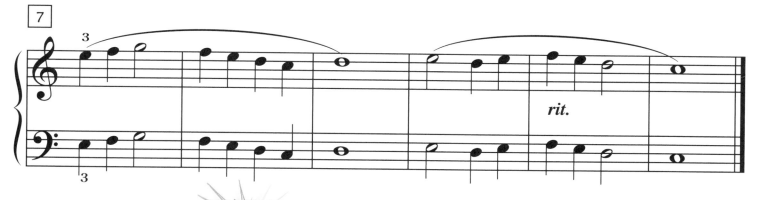

Premier Performer   *Play the RH a little louder than the LH.*

Duet: Student plays **LH** one octave higher.

Moderately   Alexander/Mier

CD 5/6
GM 3

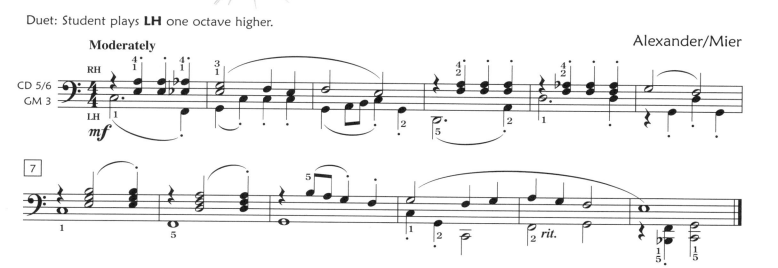

Crescendo and Diminuendo

Playing gradually louder or
gradually softer allows music to
express moods and feelings.

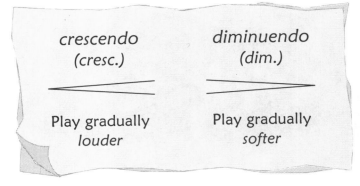

crescendo (cresc.)	diminuendo (dim.)
Play gradually *louder*	Play gradually *softer*

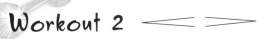

Workout 2

Play 3 times each day.

Au clair de la lune

French

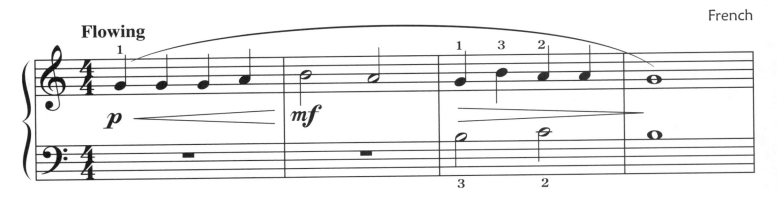

Flowing

Duet: Student plays one octave higher.

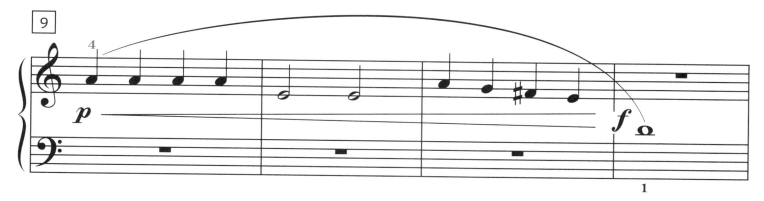

Sight-Reading

Play and say the note names as quickly as you can, once each day.
Notice the *crescendo* and *diminuendo*.

Tempo

The *tempo* is the speed of the beats in a piece of music. Italian words, written above the time signature, are often used as *tempo markings*.

Allegro = fast, quickly.

The Food Court

CD 9/10   GM 5

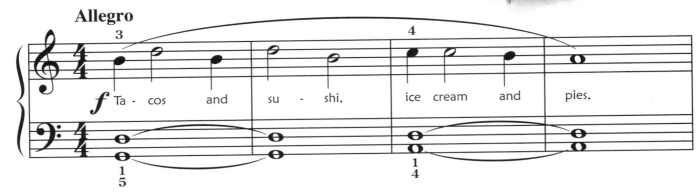

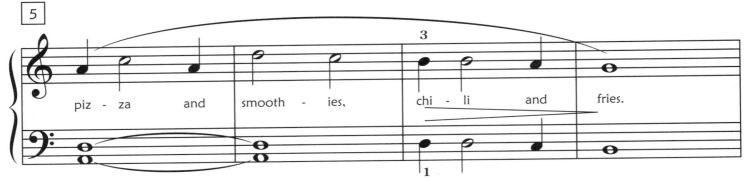

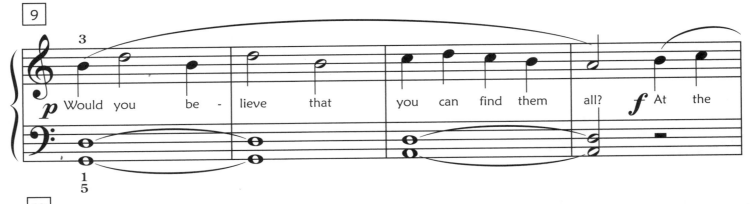

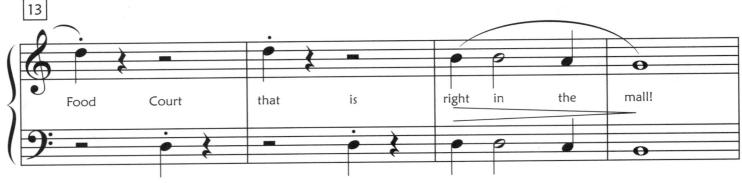

Closer Look Tap the rhythm in measures 17–18 with the correct hands. Count aloud.

Tonic (I) and Dominant (V)
of the C 5-finger Pattern

Each note of the 5-finger pattern has a name and a number, usually written as a Roman numeral.

Two of the most important notes are:

Note	Roman Numeral	Name
1st note (C)	**I** (1)	Tonic
5th note (G)	**V** (5)	Dominant

C 5-finger Pattern

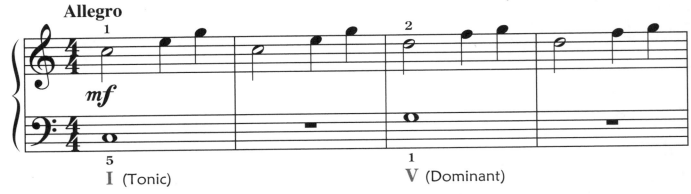

Tonic   Dominant

Tonic and Dominant

Cornelius Gurlitt (1820–1901)
Adapted from Op. 117, No. 5

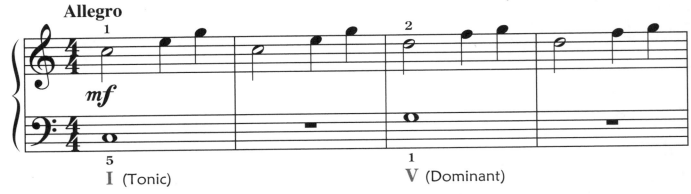

Premier Performer

Play again with the LH one octave higher, as Gurlitt originally wrote it.

Duet: Student plays one octave higher.

Alexander/Mier

Accent Sign >

To *accent* a note means
to play the note *louder*
than those before or after.

Accent signs appear *over* or *under* notes.

Shadows

CD 13/14   GM 7

Workout 3 **LH 2 over 1**

Play 3 times each day.

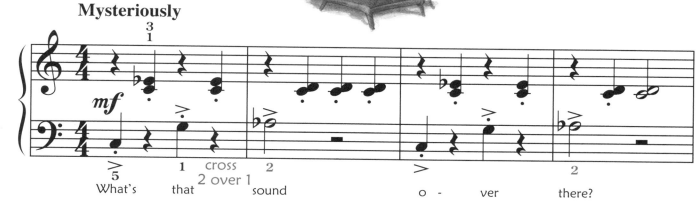

Mysteriously

What's that sound o - ver there?

I think there's a shad - ow right be - hind that chair! Let's take a

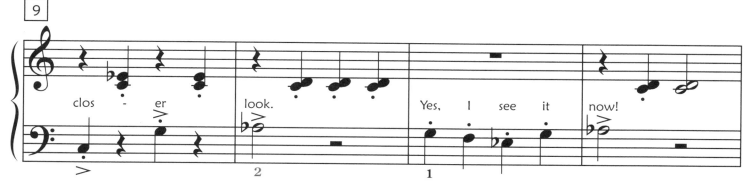

clos - er look. Yes, I see it now!

Take my hand, let's tip - toe clos - er. Eek! It is a mouse! *Run!*

Lowest C
on piano

The I Chord

in the C 5-finger Pattern

The **I** chord is built on the **1st** note (tonic) of the C 5-finger pattern.

The 1st, 3rd and 5th notes of the C 5-finger pattern are C–E–G. These notes form a **C** chord.

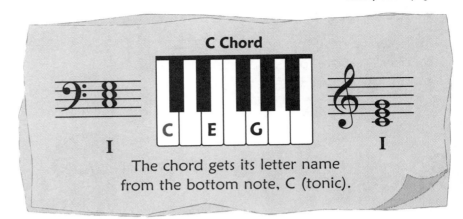

The chord gets its letter name from the bottom note, C (tonic).

Broken Chords—play one note at a time.
Block Chords—play all three notes together.

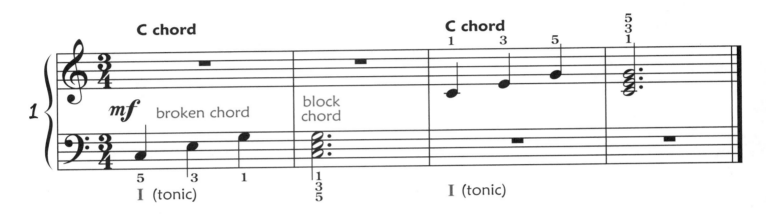

Block Chords

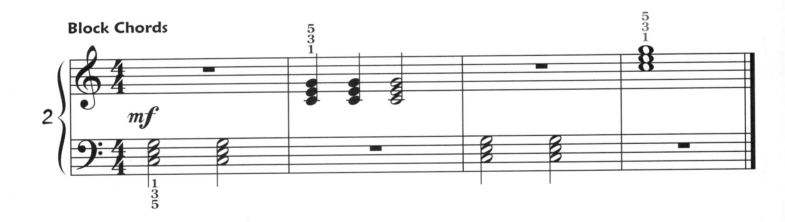

Broken Chords

Play and count aloud, once each day.

Sight-Reading

Boogie Boarding

CD 15/16 GM 8

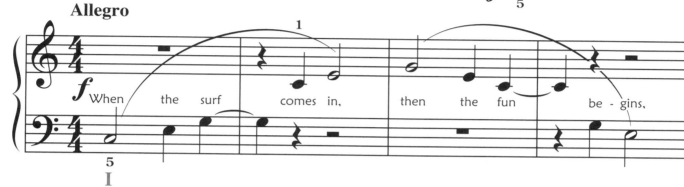

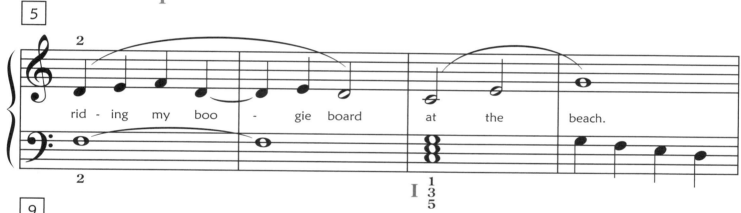

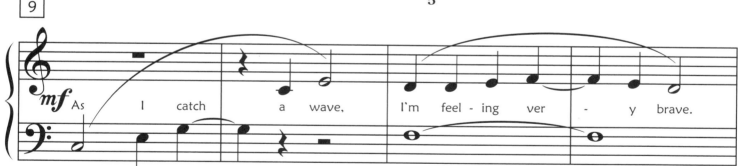

Press damper pedal and hold to end.

The V⁷ Chord

in the C 5-finger Pattern

The **V7** (5-7) chord is built on the **5th** note (dominant) of the 5-finger pattern.

The **V7** chord in C has 4 notes: G–B–D–F.

Only 2 notes of the chord (F and G played as a 2nd) will be used to play the **V7** sound in this book.

1. Play **I** and **V7**, saying the chord names aloud.

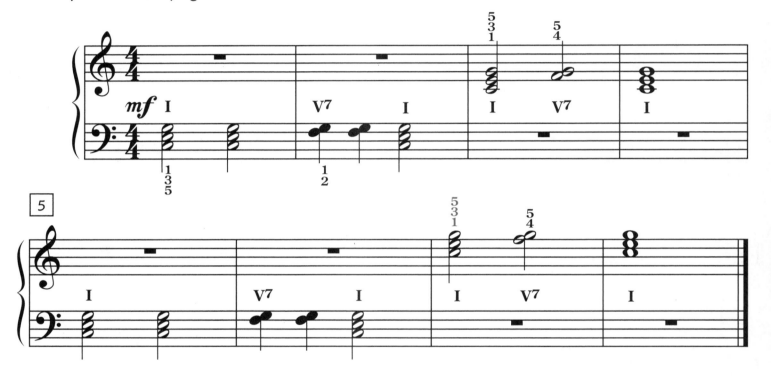

2. Using these rhythms, play **I** and **V7** in C by reading the chord symbols.

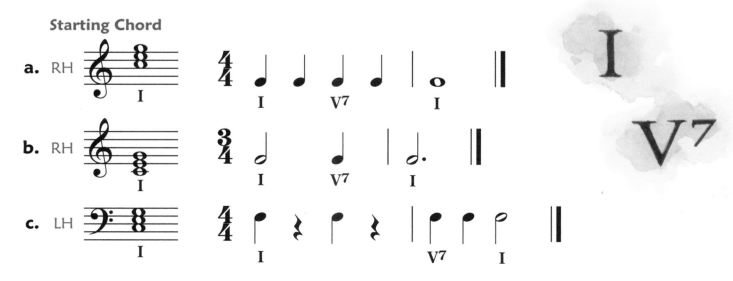

My New Skate Shoes

CD 17/18 GM 9

Allegro

I got some brand - new shoes!

Look at what they can do!

They have a wheel in each heel that I can use.

I love my new skate shoes!

Jeremiah Clarke (1673–1707) was an organist who lived in England. He composed music for church services and for plays. This is a famous, triumphant piece that is often played using trumpet, organ and drums.

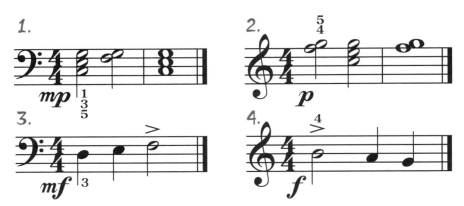

Sight-Reading
Play and count aloud, once each day.

New Tempo Marking

Moderato = play at a moderate tempo.

Trumpet Voluntary

Jeremiah Clarke

Moderato

Duet: Student plays one octave higher.

Alexander/Mier

CD 19/20
GM 10

Eighth Notes

Two eighth notes are played in the same time as one quarter note.

Count: 1   +   1   +
        (and)   (and)

Four eighth notes are played in the same time as one half note.

Count: 1 + 2 +   1 + 2 +
        (and)

Tap and count aloud (or say the words) these rhythm patterns.

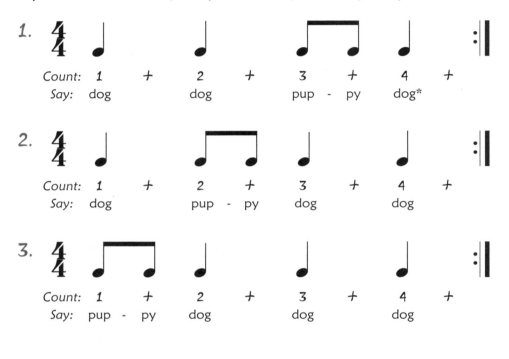

1. 4/4

Count: 1   +   2   +   3   +   4   +
Say: dog   dog   pup - py   dog*

2. 4/4

Count: 1   +   2   +   3   +   4   +
Say: dog   pup - py   dog   dog

3. 4/4

Count: 1   +   2   +   3   +   4   +
Say: pup - py   dog   dog   dog

Name That Tune!

Play these familiar Christmas melodies that use eighth notes. Can you name them?

1. 𝄞 4/4 *mf* _____

2. 𝄞 4/4 *mf* _____

Premier Performer

Play the Name That Tune! *examples again one octave lower with the LH.*

* Cat lovers may say:
  "Cat, cat, kit-ty cat," *etc.*

QWERTY*

CD 21/22 GM 11

New Rhythm

Count: 1 + 2 + 3 + 4 +

Tap and count aloud 3 times each day.

Moderato

Q and W - E - R - T - Y, as I type, my fin-gers just fly by!

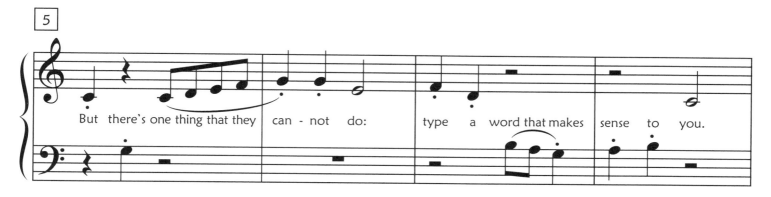

But there's one thing that they can-not do: type a word that makes sense to you.

Ev-'ry time that I try, don't know how, don't know why, I can't find X or I, B or J!

Could you teach me how to type to - day? Then my words will be A - O - K!

* QWERTY is the name for the layout of typewriter or computer keys; the first six keys of the top row of letters.

Theory Book: pages 18–19
Performance Book: pages 14–15

New Time Signature

2/4 means 2 counts in every measure.

means a quarter note ♩ gets 1 count.

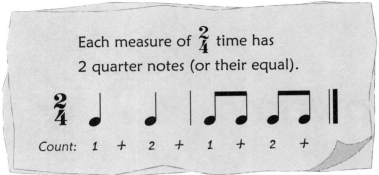

Each measure of **2/4** time has
2 quarter notes (or their equal).

Count: 1 + 2 + 1 + 2 +

Together

Moderato

mp We could ride our bikes, then read a book or two,

Duet: Student plays one octave higher.

Moderato

CD 23/24
GM 12

p *simile*

⑤

⑨ ⑬

A little slower

⑰

rit.

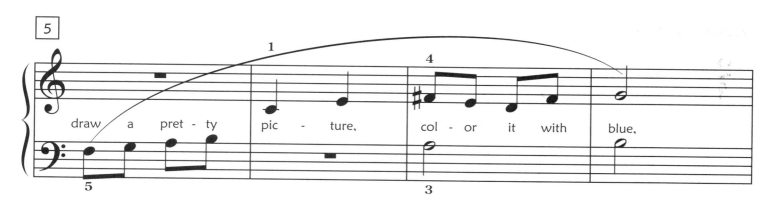

draw a pret - ty pic - ture, col - or it with blue,

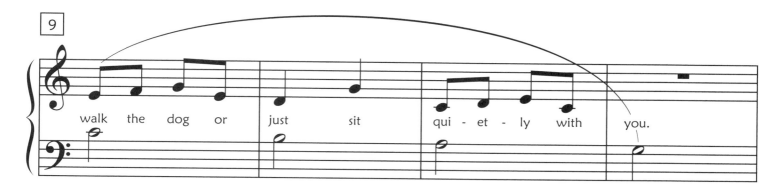

walk the dog or just sit qui - et - ly with you.

You can choose what - ev - er you want to do.

A little slower

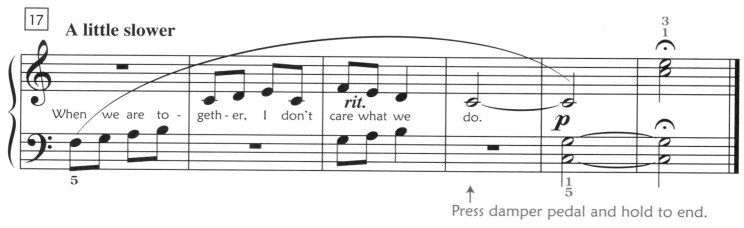

When we are to - geth - er, I don't care what we do.

rit. *p*

↑
Press damper pedal and hold to end.

Premier Performer   *Listen to make the melody very legato.*

8va Lower

When placed *below* the staff, *8va* means to play one octave (8 notes) lower than written.

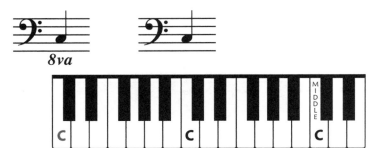

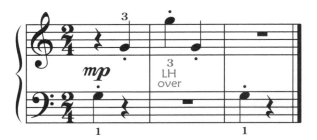

Play 3 times each day.

Folk Song Mix-Up

(Do Your Ears Hang Low?/Turkey in the Straw)

CD 25/26 GM 13

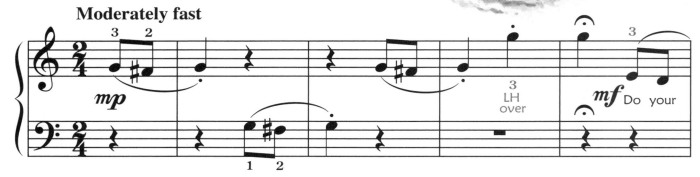

Imagination Station

Play by ear another folk song that you know, such as Twinkle, Twinkle, Little Star. Your teacher can help you.

Natural Sign

A *natural sign* is the music symbol that cancels a previous sharp or flat. The note following a natural sign is *always* a white key.

Workout 5 Playing a Natural

Play 3 times each day.

Homework

CD 27/28 GM 14

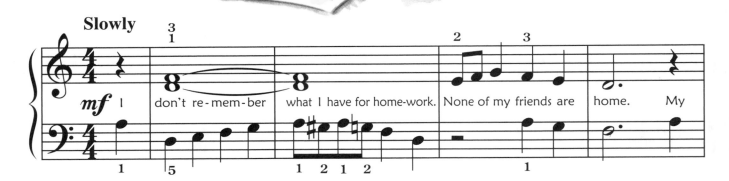

Slowly

I don't re-mem-ber what I have for home-work. None of my friends are home. My

5

mom says there is no more tel-e-vi-sion, and I can't use the phone. *p* I

9

al-ways write it all down in my note-book, but to-day I just for-got. *mf* There's

13

one thing I re-mem-ber 'bout my home-work: I know I have a lot!

Workout 6 Moving Naturally

Play 3 times each day.

Movin' On

CD 29/30 GM 15

Press damper pedal and hold to end.

28

Tonic (I) and Dominant (V)
of the G 5-finger Pattern

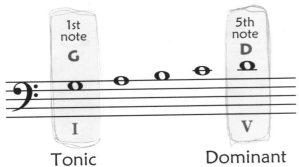

Tonic   Dominant

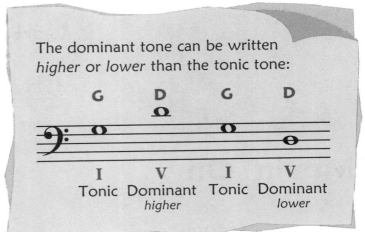

The dominant tone can be written *higher* or *lower* than the tonic tone:

Minuet

CD 31/32 GM 16

Alexander Reinagle
(1756–1809)

The I Chord

in the G 5-finger Pattern

The **I** chord is built on the **1st** note (tonic) of the G 5-finger pattern.

The 1st, 3rd and 5th notes of the G 5-finger pattern are G–B–D. These notes form a **G** chord.

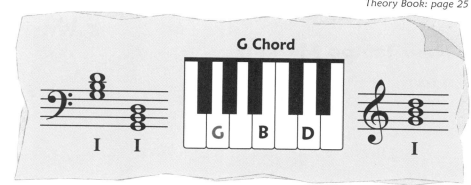

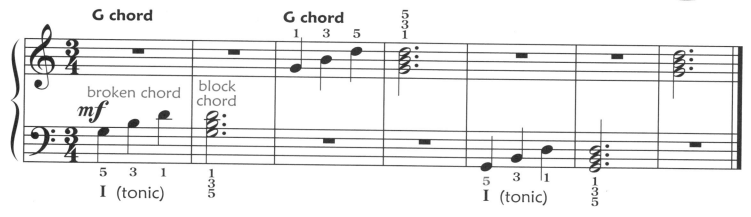

The V⁷ Chord

in the G 5-finger Pattern

The **V7** chord in G has 4 notes: D–F♯–A–C.

Only 2 notes of the chord (C and D played as a 2nd) will be used to play the **V7** sound in this book.

Play **I** and **V7**, saying the names aloud.

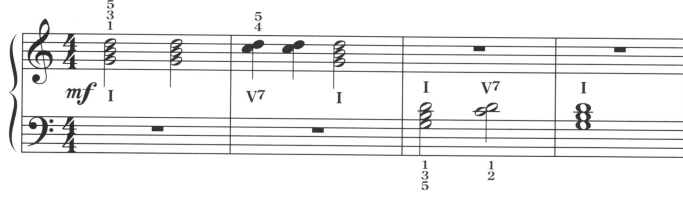

New Tempo Marking

a tempo = return to previous tempo;
often follows *ritardando (rit.)*

Workout 7 **Legato and Staccato**

Play 3 times each day.

Tilt-a-Whirl

CD 33/34 GM 17

Moderato

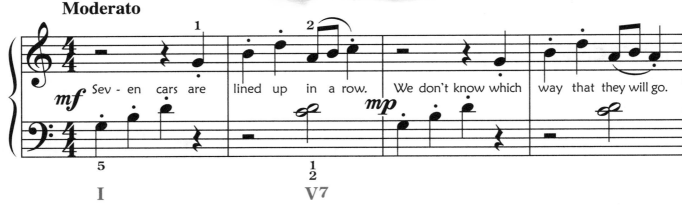

Sev - en cars are lined up in a row. We don't know which way that they will go.

I   V7

Front-wards, back-wards, spin - ning up and down, Tilt - a - Whirl, twirl-ing a - round. This

I

Name notes.

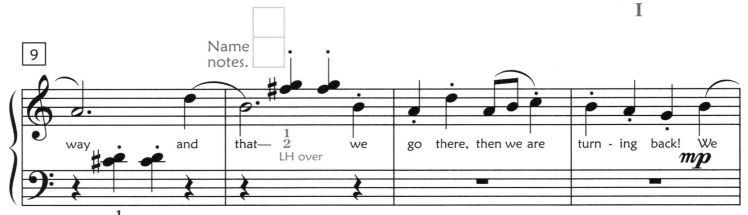

way   and that— we go there, then we are turn - ing back! We

LH over

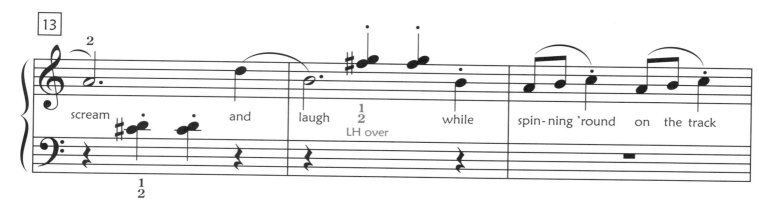

13

scream and laugh while spin-ning 'round on the track

16

high and low, to and fro. When the ride starts to slow, then we let go.

rit.

19

a tempo

Hur-ry! Let's run and get back in line. We all want to ride an-oth-er time.

23

Front-wards, back-wards, spin-ning up and down, Tilt-a-Whirl, twirl-ing a - round.

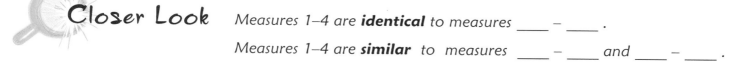

Closer Look *Measures 1–4 are **identical** to measures ____ – ____ .*

*Measures 1–4 are **similar** to measures ____ – ____ and ____ – ____ .*

Pedal Sign

The pedal on the right is the damper pedal.
When it is held down, tones continue to sound
after the keys have been released.

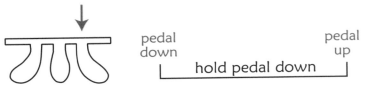

pedal
down

pedal
up

hold pedal down

The Gymnast

Reminder: When
using the pedal,
keep your heel on
the floor. Adjust the
bench if needed.

CD 35/36 GM 18

Gracefully

f Watch the gym-nast on the bal-ance beam as she stands up on her toes.

Pedal down

Hold pedal down

She has worked so hard on her rou-tine and it real-ly shows. mf For

Pedal up

nine-ty sec-onds she must turn and flip with-out a wob-ble or a slip. And mp

Pedal down

Pedal up

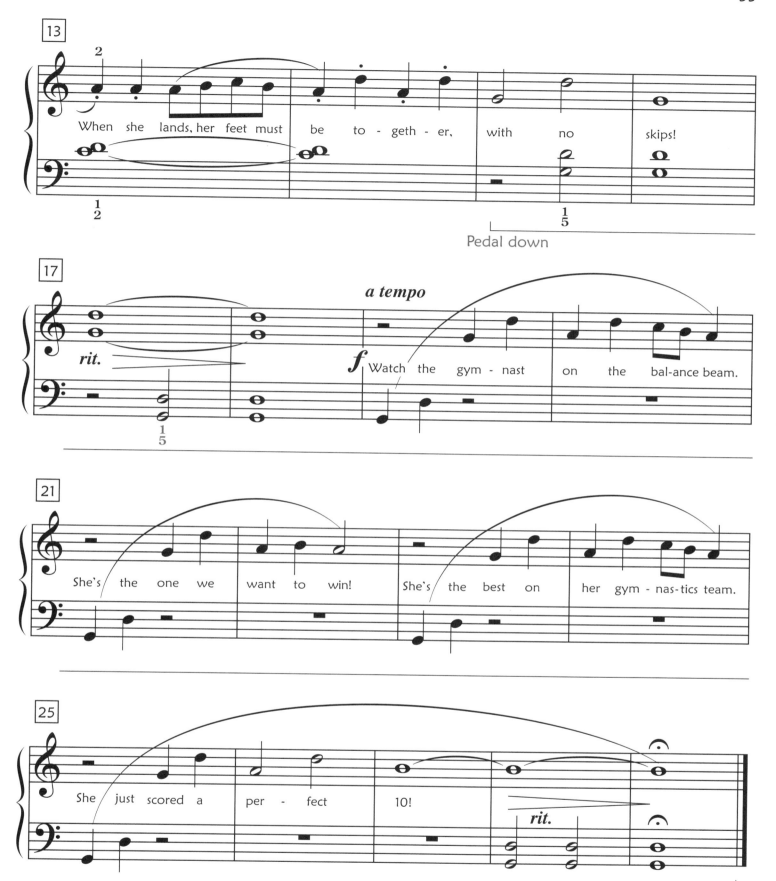

13
When she lands, her feet must be to-geth-er, with no skips!

17
a tempo
rit.
f Watch the gym - nast on the bal-ance beam.

21
She's the one we want to win! She's the best on her gym - nas-tics team.

25
She just scored a per - fect 10!
rit.

Pedal down

Pedal and hands lift
at the same time.

Closer Look Circle each melodic 4th in The Gymnast.

Half Step

A half step is the distance from one key to the *very next* key, whether black or white.

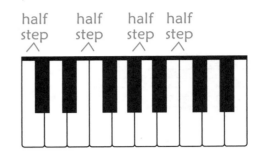

A sharp sign ♯ *raises* a note a half step (to the right).

A flat sign ♭ *lowers* a note a half step (to the left).

Each black key has two names— a sharp name and a flat name.

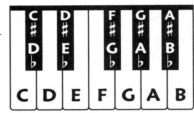

Playing Half Steps

1. Play 𝄢 ○ 3   then play the note that is **up** a half step. Name the note: ____♯ or ____♭

2. Play 𝄞 ○ 2   then play the note that is **up** a half step. Name the note: ____♯ or ____♭

3. Play 𝄢 ○ 2   then play the note that is **down** a half step. Name the note: ____♯ or ____♭

4. Play 𝄞 ○ 3   then play the note that is **down** a half step. Name the note: ____♯ or ____♭

Sight-Reading   Play and count aloud, once each day.

1.

2.

3.

4.

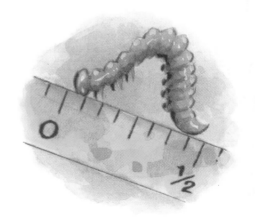

Half-Way There

(A Study of Half Steps)

CD 37/38 GM 19

Workout 8 **Half Steps Up and Down**

Play 3 times each day.

Moderato

When we're on a fam - 'ly road trip we get bored in the car.

5

Then my broth - er asks our fa - ther, "Are we there yet? Is it far?"

9

Min - utes seem like days, each day lasts a year— this whole road trip is not fair!

13

Then our dad says what we're dread - ing, "We are on - ly half - way there!"

Whole Step

A whole step is equal to 2 half steps. Play two keys with *one* black or white key between.

1 whole step = 2 half steps

C# (D♭)
between

G
between

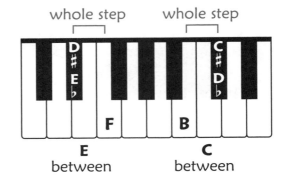

E
between

C
between

Playing Whole Steps

1. Play  then play the note that is **up** a whole step. Name the note: _____

2. Play  then play the note that is **up** a whole step. Name the note: _____

3. Play  then play the note that is **down** a whole step. Name the note: ♭

4. Play  then play the note that is **down** a whole step. Name the note: _____

Whole Steps Only

CD 39/40 GM 20

Transposition

Playing the same music starting on a different note from the original is called *transposition*. The notes are different, but the *intervals* are the same.

Premier Performer *Transpose to D. Each hand will begin on D.*

The Ocean Deep

(A Study of Whole Steps)

CD 41/42 GM 21

Theory Book: page 31
Performance Book: pages 24–25

Slowly and mysteriously

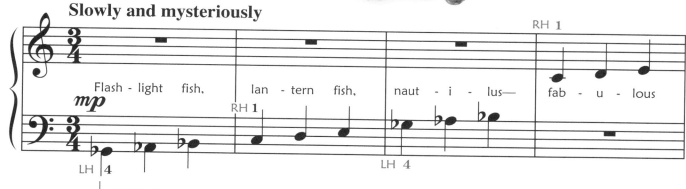

Flash - light fish, lan - tern fish, naut - i - lus— fab - u - lous

crea - tures that thrive where there's no light.

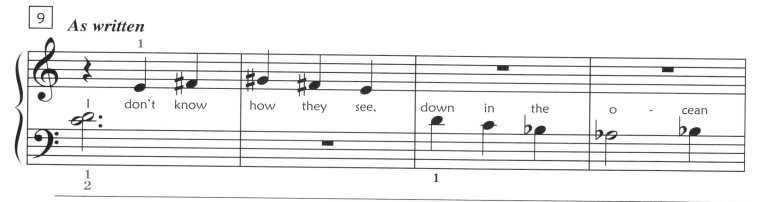

As written

I don't know how they see, down in the o - cean

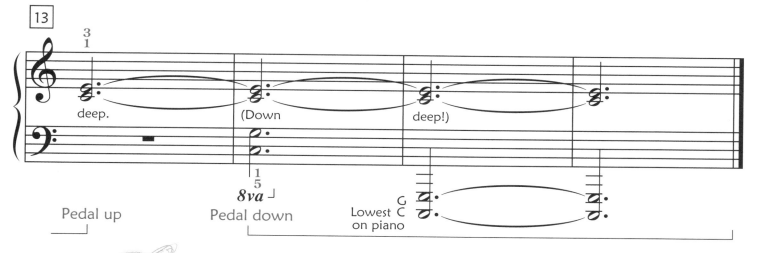

deep. (Down deep!)

Pedal up   Pedal down   Lowest C on piano   G

🪐 Imagination Station

Using the notes in measures 3–4 of The Ocean Deep, create your own whole-step piece.

Major 5-Finger Patterns

with All White Keys

The *major* 5-finger pattern is formed when the tonic note (**I**) is followed by a

whole step—whole step—half step—whole step

Play the following major patterns hands separately, then together.

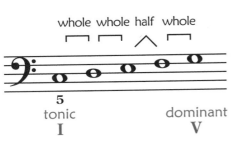
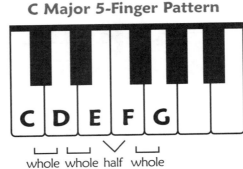

C Major 5-Finger Pattern

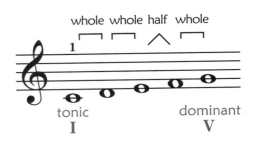

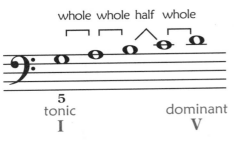
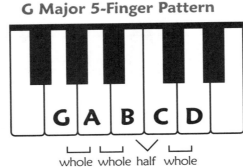

G Major 5-Finger Pattern

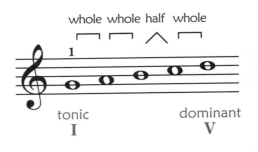

C Major 5-Finger Pattern and Chords

Play hands together. Then transpose to the G major 5-finger pattern.

Premier Performer

Transpose Bartók's Study on page 7 to the G major 5-finger pattern.

Major 5-Finger Patterns
with 1 Black Key in the Middle

Play the following major patterns hands separately, then together.

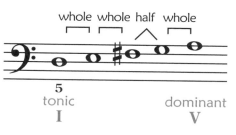

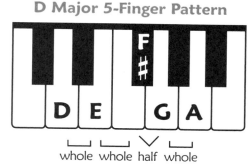

D Major 5-Finger Pattern

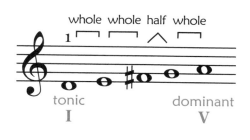

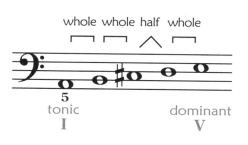

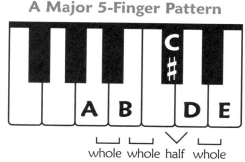

A Major 5-Finger Pattern

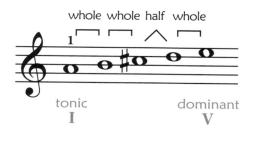

D Major 5-Finger Pattern and Chords

Play hands together. Then transpose to the A major 5-finger pattern.

Premier Performer *Transpose Bartok's Study on page 7 to the D major 5-finger pattern; then to the A major 5-finger pattern.*

The V7 Chord
in the D 5-finger Pattern

The **V7** chord in D has 4 notes: A–C#–E–G. Only 2 notes of the chord (G and A played as a 2nd) will be used to play a **V7** sound in this book.

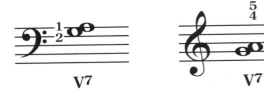

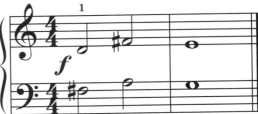

Workout 9 Hands Together

Play 3 times each day.

The Autograph

CD 43/44 GM 22

Moderately fast

I can't wait to show my friends what I just got!

When we were out to - day, just walk - ing a - long the way, I

thought that I saw my fav - 'rite mov - ie star.

Premier Performer *Transpose measures 1–4 to the A major 5-finger pattern.*

Interval of a 6th

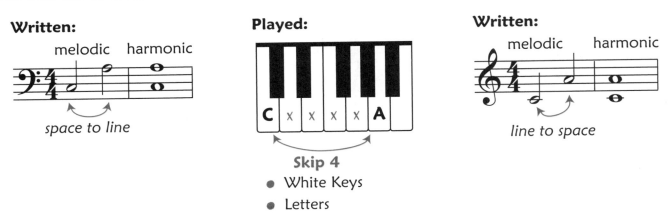

Written: melodic harmonic
space to line

Played:
C x x x x A
Skip 4
- White Keys
- Letters

Written: melodic harmonic
line to space

Listen as you play melodic and harmonic 6ths. Stretch the hand slightly to play a 6th.

Name notes

Name notes

Growing

CD 45/46 GM 23

Moderato

mf If I stand up real - ly tall, make a mark on the wall,

5

take a yard - stick, meas - ure twice— grow - ing up is nice!
rit.

8va

Workout 10 Moving 6ths

Play 3 times each day.

Classic Dance

CD 47/48 GM 24

Stately and unhurried

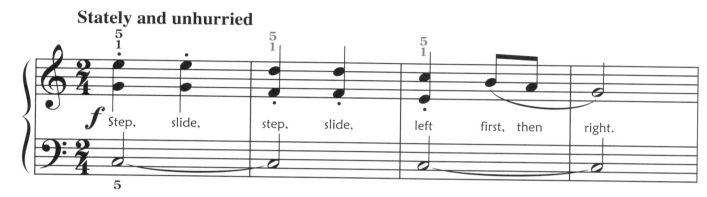

f Step, slide, step, slide, left first, then right.

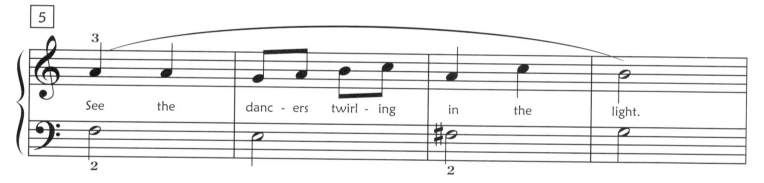

See the danc-ers twirl-ing in the light.

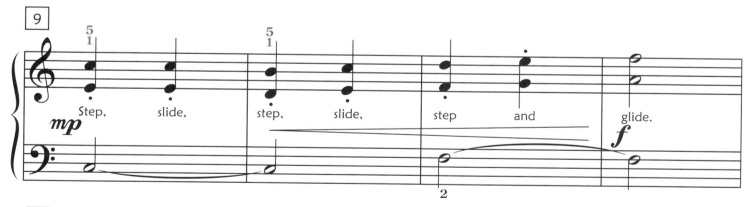

mp Step, slide, step, slide, step and glide. *f*

turn-ing so grace-ful-ly, side by side.

Theory Book: pages 38–39
Performance Book: pages 28–29

Sight-Reading   Play and count aloud, once each day.

Rainy Day Blues

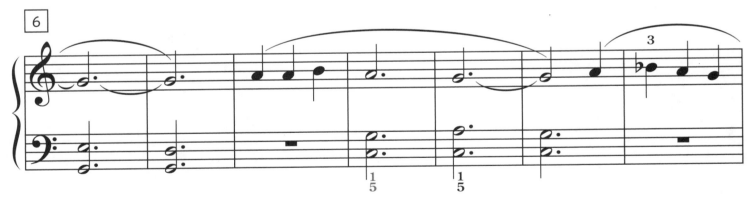

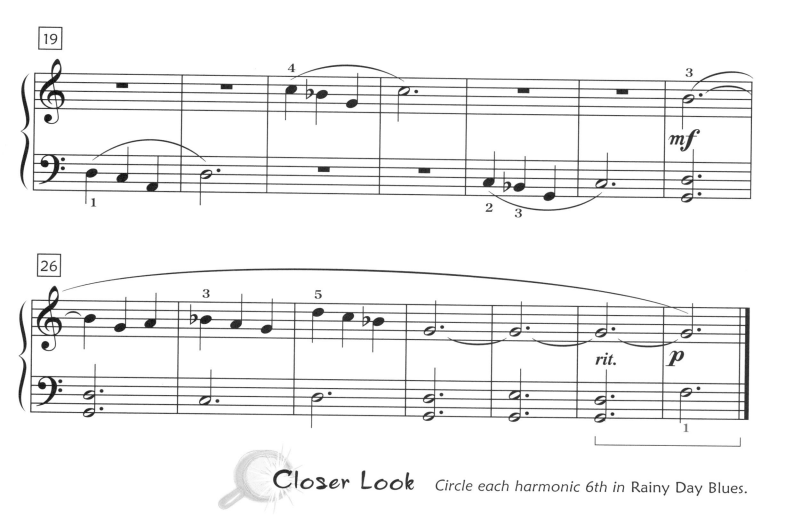

Closer Look *Circle each harmonic 6th in Rainy Day Blues.*

Duet: Student does not play pedal with duet in measures 31–32.

Theory Book: page 40
Performance Book: pages 30-31

Telling a Story with Music

Many things help pianists tell a story through music.

- The sentence at the beginning of each section of *King Arthur's Adventure* will help you use your imagination as you play.

- Changes in tempo and dynamics create new feelings and emotions.

- Pedal adds interest and color to the sound.

- Playing *staccato* and *legato* helps create different scenes and moods.

King Arthur's* Adventure

CD 51/52 GM 26

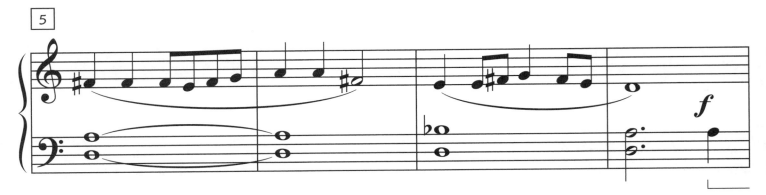

* King Arthur was a mythical English king who led the famous Knights of the Round Table.

13

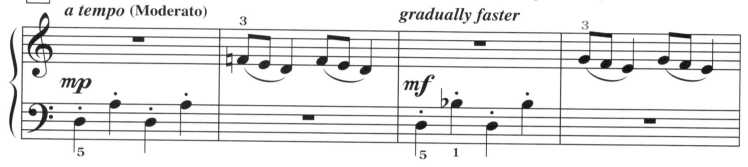

17 *(The horses and riders gallop faster and faster to rescue the fair young maiden.)*

a tempo **(Moderato)**   ***gradually faster***

mp   mf

21 **Allegro**

f

(King Arthur and his knights return to the castle, victorious.)

25 *(The fair maiden is now safe.)*   **Moderato**

rit.   f

8va

Closer Look

*Circle two tempo markings—*allegro *and* moderato— *in* King Arthur's Adventure. *Observe them as you play.*

Alfred's Premier Performer

Piano Achievement Award

presented to

_____

Student

You have

successfully completed

Lesson Book 2A

and are

hereby promoted to

Lesson Book 2B.

_____   _____

Teacher   *Date*